3 0132 02546223 0

D1757037

Books are to be returned on or before
the last date below.

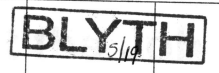

Contents

Introduction

The inspiration behind this book came about whilst I was on holiday in Spain over Christmas 2018 reflecting on another year of mixed fortunes work-wise, and a lifetime comprising of hundreds of interviews and scores of temporary and permanent roles, some of which ended by my own volition with blistering resignation letters that are too good to keep to myself.

I have more or less skipped over the aspect of searching for that elusive job you are seeking as most individuals are pretty savvy in job-hunting. Instead, I have cut to the chase and focused on securing an interview, the preparation before the interview, the interview itself in nailing the job you want and how to set the bar when it comes to resigning from the job you have come to hate, knowing you deserve so much better.

I have the power and ability to craft letters in minutes that are razor sharp, factual, straight to the point and succinct with content that cannot be doubted or questioned.

I wrote and published a consumer book in September 2016 that has plenty of 5* reviews on Amazon and has sold on 3 continents. *How to Effectively Resolve Consumer Complaints and Motoring Disputes* spans various consumer laws over 3 jurisdictions (England and Wales, Scotland and the Isle of Man).

I also built and host a popular consumer website that neatly links in with my book www.thegrumpygit.com, which attracts a lot of global traffic. I have published over 90 blogs spanning various consumer matters of interest as well as a few random blogs inspired by chance conversations and experiences. I use this as a platform to convey my thoughts and musings to a global audience on topics that people find factual, engaging and enjoyable to read.

People who have a way with words are described as 'wordsmiths' and whilst I have been called many things over the years, the one thing that people keep saying to me is that I have a unique way with words that can illustrate and illuminate in equal measure.

Actions may speak louder than words, but I can find the right adjectives and metaphors to portray meaning and capture a scenario succinctly.

My website that I use to showcase my writing is www.awriterinedinburgh.com.

I hope you find this book informative, funny, engaging and an enjoyable read.

Part 1

How to Get the Job You Want

Cover Letter

A concise, well written cover letter will set your application apart from other applicants in capturing the attention of your future employer from the outset, and research suggests that you increase your chances by about 47% in securing an interview with a good cover letter.

Every role is different, even within the same firm, so it is imperative that your cover letter is tailored to suit the specific role you are applying for. This is your opportunity to impress the individual who is vetting the applications before they even read your CV.

Find out who to personally address the letter to rather than a generic 'Dear Sir / Madam' to ensure your application is considered and noticed for the right reasons. This can be found in the job advert or by searches on LinkedIn or Google.

In the first paragraph, state the role that you wish to be considered for and why you are applying for the role.

In the second paragraph, elaborate on why you would like to work for this firm and convey your knowledge and passion you share, complete with your knowledge of the company. A good way to connect with your prospective employer is to express that you share their values and ethos and that you would be a great ambassador in promoting these if you were hired and aspire to exceed their set targets and goals.

You could clearly bullet point the skills, expertise and work experience that the employer requires in this section.

The third paragraph is where you focus on your skills and experience relevant to the job advert. It is paramount that you match your skills to what this role requires as well as the fact that you are adaptable and can easily learn whatever is required to perform effectively in the role.

You can encapsulate the strengths you have gathered throughout your life on a professional and personal level that would add value to the role and business holistically. It is useful to throw in some examples of outside hobbies and interests that capture your strengths at this point, simply to convey that you are a rounded individual who is adaptable and one that fits in well with individuals from all walks of life.

Your final paragraph should wrap up your letter succinctly, thanking your prospective employer for taking the time to read your letter and that you look forward to hearing from them.

One template that I use to craft my cover letters is given below;

Dear X,

I wish to apply for the role of (X) as advertised on your website.

I am familiar with effective time management by virtue of various roles primarily in financial services where I have had to identify and effectively manage risk to time-driven deadlines.

I have a good working knowledge of Word and intermediate Excel skills, which is demonstrated from my work as a professional writer and author in tandem with a popular consumer website I host that attracts plenty of global traffic. I manage my own publishing firm, prepare the accounts and keep the statutory records in good order.

My last role at (firm)... (describe role and responsibilities).

I would relish the opportunity to work with a well-respected firm and employer of choice that can offer a structured career progression and apply my varied skills set to benefit your firm and clients.

I am seeking a full-time permanent position and my current salary is £X + benefits with a 1-week notice period.

I would welcome the opportunity to meet you at a mutually convenient time to discuss my CV, and I look forward to hearing from you soon.

Yours sincerely,

Social Media

Current research suggests that 70% of recruiters look at social media profiles of applicants on Facebook and LinkedIn before considering inviting an applicant to an interview and about 43% of employers use social media to check on current employees. A similar number of employers have actually sourced a candidate through social media.

Almost all employers (93% is the figure given) vet applicants via social media during the interview process. Therefore, it's imperative you ensure your profiles project the right impression based on what you post and the type of photos you share; all of which can be found in the public domain.

Employers are looking for candidates who are creative and social and will be screening out those they consider as having inappropriate online behaviour. Whilst that is subjective, it's something you need to be aware of. Do an online search in the guise of a prospective employer on your own name (using inverted commas to narrow down searches on your name only 'John Smith' home town, etc).

If you wouldn't want your mother to see what you have posted, would you want an employer to see the same content? Whilst you are entitled to your views and opinions, you have the right to remain silent. You do not have to say anything but it may harm your defence if you do not answer when questioned something which you rely on in court and anything you do say may be given in evidence (as the police say). Employers want to see you using common sense.

CV

One thing I have learnt over the years is that it's not the best person who secures the job above all others; it is the one who has simply sold the best script by virtue of a well-crafted CV complete with the art of bullshitting.

Whilst blatant lying is frowned upon, embellishing the truth demonstrates to recruiters that you may possess some of the most highly sought-after skills in corporate environments. A lack of honesty and integrity, and being a bullshitter scores highly. Bullshitting skills are in high demand and authenticity is frowned upon. Behaving naturally in many work environments is either seen as a display of rebellion or madness.

The only thing that counts here is who wins, so embellishing the truth particularly on your achievements is a good thing because it helps you win. The majority of the most 'successful' people I have known have been pathetic on nearly every level except for their capacity for bullshitting, lying, intrigue and general dishonesty. This equates to success.

So you need to craft your CV around the job description to stand a decent chance of being shortlisted. Whilst you can't change the facts about your employment history, there's no harm in overegging the pudding on what you achieved in each role.

One individual springs to mind here. He worked for 4 weeks in a role before I came along and stated that he wrote the procedures for the department, when in actual fact he cobbled together about 4–5 pages at a push about how to do the most elementary of tasks before moving on to pastures new. Will anyone question that? Probably not. I wrote 43 pages in 10 weeks for the same role before resigning yet my 'manager' (I use that word loosely) claimed he didn't have time in about 6 years to do anything at all. It's a great example of bullshitting as it sounds plausible and nobody will think of questioning it.

Overegg the pudding and list your achievements in your roles, even if it's not completely truthful, so long as it can't be questioned or verified. References from most organisations simply confirm the basics and nobody is going to ask for evidence that you exceeded set targets with specific percentages. This is what HR want to see and the best bullshitter wins the prize.

How to Organise your CV

Employers may only have about 30 seconds to read a CV and are looking for applicants who match the job description in order to interview them. Therefore, your CV must be focussed and tell an employer what they need to know insofar as you having the skills, strengths and experience which enable you to do the job that they are advertising.

You want your CV to give a Hiring Manager / Talent Acquisition Manager (or whatever else they call themselves nowadays) a brief overview of your background and experience to convince them you are worth inviting for an interview where you can then talk about your skills in more detail. A lot of firms actually use software and algorithms to search for keywords to filter CVs, so your cover letter and CV need to contain the keywords to get shortlisted.

General Tips

Your skills, work experience, education and strengths relevant for the job should be on the front page and preferably in your personal statement. All information here should be relevant and recent.

Always focus your CV on the kind of work you are aiming for. Use the initial profile and skills section to do this (your work experience and education will generally remain the same).

Make sure your CV includes enough detail about job-specific competencies, but avoid unnecessary detail and aim to have no more than 2 pages.

Use narrower margins to give more width for text. I usually use a 1.27cm margin on all 4 sides.

Do not include a photograph, National Insurance number, passport number, marital status, number of children, religion or nationality. You are not required to include your date of birth and it is recommended that you do not use a font size of less than 10 point.

Do not print on coloured paper.

Do not use a coloured font.

Do not include GCSEs or a high school education if your age deems it irrelevant.

Do not include interests and hobbies unless it directly relates to the vacancy as they are not relevant for most employers.

Employers are unlikely to have the time to visit websites / blogs given to them by applicants and indeed this can be seen as 'lazy' by not putting the relevant information on the CV itself, so I would suggest not including them.

Treat voluntary work as if it were paid employment.

Write in the present tense and use action or 'doing' words.

Finally, double check your CV for grammatical and spelling errors.

Keep your CV saved on all electronic devices for ease of reference and ad-hoc job applications that you may wish to submit.

The following is a guide to sections to include on a CV

Personal Details

Name

Address and postcode

Telephone number

E-mail address

Career Aim / Personal Profile / Introduction / Career Summary

This section can be changed depending on the job vacancy and this is your USP (Unique Selling Point).

A brief, positive summary of your abilities and experience in relation to work you are seeking. Try to keep this introductory paragraph within 80–100 words to convince a recruiter to continue reading your CV.

Use keywords in the job specification to describe yourself.

Back up statements with facts. Saying, *"I have proven ability to easily adapt to change in any situation by virtue of successfully completing various assignments / projects with (employer)"* instead of saying, *"I work well within teams"* has more impact.

Employers are tired of seeing 'catch all' statements from candidates who state that they can work well on their own and as part of a team and they take it as a given that you are a good communicator, so avoid saying this.

Key Skills / Relevant Skills / Achievements / Personal Qualities

This section can be changed depending on the job vacancy and this again is your USP. You ought to focus on the transferable skills you have gained from your career, although you can consider other skills from your personal life, volunteering projects and interests if you need to.

Start with the skills you have which are relevant to the job you are applying for and bullet point your key personal strengths and core personal attributes. To save space you could compile the bullet points into two columns as a table.

Whilst hard skills are always going to be important, it's the soft skills that enable you to be adaptable. Research suggests that 57% of senior leaders say that soft skills are more important than hard skills. An increased use of Artificial Intelligence (AI) in the workplace means that there will be more importance placed on this in years to come.

Creativity is the most in-demand soft skill as organisations need creative employees who can craft future solutions needed to drive the business forward. Demonstrating your creativity essentially suggests that you are curious and innovative, you will play a key role in problem solving and be instrumental in thinking of new ideas with independence of mind and clarity of thought.

Highlighting successful ideas and concepts demonstrates your ability to positively improve your knowledge and it sets you apart from other candidates.

You need to ensure that your hard and soft skills are constantly up-to-date to stay relevant so whenever you learn a new skill, remember to update your CV and LinkedIn profile. Don't forget to add these keywords to your CV in a way which will ensure it passes the algorithms and on to the shortlist.

Human skills matter and you need to come across as having the right mix of hard and soft skills needed to work effectively, combined with emerging technology. Being adaptable to change and showing you can clearly deliver value in today's ever-changing world of work is the key to setting you apart from other applicants.

Work Experience / Career History / Employment History

Start with your most recent job and work backwards or most relevant.

Give the name of the employer and where they are located (no need to include full postal address), the dates you worked there, the job title and a brief description of duties. Just keep the description to a summary sentence of what the role was and 3 – 4 bullet points of typical tasks and duties.

List your key achievements with specific percentages if necessary to demonstrate that you are head and shoulders above the rest, even if it's untrue. It's hardly going to be questioned so long as it's plausible.

Use action verbs to add and quantify your results and achievements and highlight your strengths. For example, try using verbs such as 'directed', 'guided', 'motivated', 'recruited' and 'engaged' instead of writing that you managed a team.

Describe your strong communication skills by using verbs like 'wrote', 'published', 'edited' or 'influenced'. This will help your CV stand out and illustrates your potential to succeed in a new role.

Many employers will look for evidence of people skills to ensure you will fit well with the team. This is not something that companies can easily teach new staff and they invariably don't want to waste time, money and resources in doing so. Take a fresh look over your employment history and consider who you dealt with, who you supported, how many were in the team, how was the primary style of communication (in person / in writing / by phone) and mention it in some of your roles.

Include part-time jobs and any unpaid voluntary work experience.

Education and Training

Consider bullet pointing and formatting this section for clarity and to keep the information concise.

Start with the most recent first or most relevant with the qualification achieved, dates that can be verified and any distinguished results and highlights.

Include school qualifications if recent and relevant.

Training details are particularly important for technical work to show that you are up-to-date with latest developments.

Leave out education details if they are not appropriate.

Additional Information

Driving licence (provisional or full) if you have one and it is relevant.

Your interests (brief details only) but only if they are relevant for the role.

References

Simply state 'references available on request' or don't even mention it as any prospective employers will seek references anyway.

Before the Interview

Fail to prepare, prepare to fail is the motto to live by here and it's essential that you do your due diligence on the firm and discreetly on the individuals who are going to be leading it.

I always look at Glassdoor (www.glassdoor.co.uk), which is basically the TripAdvisor of employers where current and former employees leave honest appraisals which are generally 'on target' and are a good benchmark as to what you can expect. If a firm is scoring anything less than 3 out of 5 on here, it's a red flag and one to give a wide berth. However, this can vary widely in a relatively short space of time. Let me explain.

I recall being successful in an interview with a firm that was scoring nearly 4 out of 5 on Glassdoor at the time. This was a positive insofar as this firm appeared to be a good employer. However, just 3 months into my probation period this score had slipped to 2.9 without any input from me.

It's worth doing anonymous searches on LinkedIn to see the background of those who will be conducting the interviews so you can see how long they have been in their respective roles and to show evidence that you have done your homework in the course of the ongoing conversation.

Before you even set off for the interview, it's worth doing a 'dry run' to ensure you know where the office is so you can arrive unflustered and prepared on the day.

This is the checklist I adhere to;

- clean shoes (it's the first thing an interviewer notices)
- pen, paper, CV, list of questions to ask and a crib sheet to refresh your memory on the firm and the names of the interviewers
- copy of the job specification
- passport, utility bill or bank statement issued within the past 3 months and proof of right to work (HMRC tax code with NI number on it or something similar)
- umbrella
- loose change for bus fares, parking fares and refreshments
- fully charged mobile phone (put on silent upon arrival)

It goes without saying you need to demonstrate that you know something about the firm to illustrate your interest in working for them, so have a quick look at their website and memorise a few key facts. I always like to find one obscure fact to throw in at the interview, one that nobody would ever know. I remember being asked what I knew about a particular firm during one of my many interviews, only to recite the usual stuff from their website in addition to saying that Alexander Graham Bell who invented the telephone was born in this office. It may have impressed the interviewers but I didn't get the job!

I am always curious to know how the position has come about, and this is a question you can ask either during the interview or in the closing questions. There's no harm in actually trying to find out by either asking someone 'in the know', or through Google searches to see how often the role has been advertised in the past or simply by trusting your gut instinct.

Always take a copy of your CV with you in a folder with some writing paper, a pen and some questions to close at the end and have this laid out in front of you from the outset to illustrate that you are well prepared and mean business.

Think of examples where you have displayed the competencies in question that are relevant for the job you are being interviewed for. Prepare beforehand and have as many examples as possible so you can convey this at the interview. You may find it useful to pencil in some keywords and prompts against various roles on your CV so you can quickly respond to the popular questions.

Researching industry articles and being aware of current trends and what the competitors are doing will give you the edge on demonstrating your interest and awareness and will help you craft some questions to convey that.

Remember, an interview cuts both ways and it's not all about them. If anything, this is about you and don't be afraid to nail your colours to the mast. Shy kids get nothing and those with the confidence, clear cut answers and who appear to be the best person for the job will secure the role.

You need to know what the salary parameters are for the job so you can give a solid answer to any closing questions about your salary expectations. This is always a tricky one to gauge, but bearing in mind the majority of these firms that are hiring will spend more on stamps and stationery in a year than your salary there's no need to sell yourself short here. Just know your worth and close by saying that you're just being honest and open here, knowing what the parameters are and what you can bring to the party. They will respect you for it rather than if you were to fluff an answer and say you are happy to negotiate and know what the pay range is.

Brass balls every time and they won't thank or respect you for underselling yourself at this juncture. They can only say "no", and you get what you pay for, whether it's a pair of shoes or a candidate.

You are the solution they are seeking to address their problems, so know your worth and lay it on the line with confidence and no waffle. This is your closing point at the end of the interview, although I have slotted it in here because you need to have this prepared before the interview to complete the circle.

Negative factors to watch for

Your potential employer will be evaluating your negative factors as well as your positive attributes, and the following points are generally considered to be the most frequent aspects that lead to rejection;

- poor personal appearance
- overbearing, aggressive or conceited 'superiority complex' and a 'know it all' demeanour
- inability to clearly express your thoughts or grammar
- lack of planning for career with no purpose or goals
- lack of interest and enthusiasm demonstrated by being passive and indifferent
- lack of confidence and nervousness

- over-emphasis on the remuneration
- evasive answers and excuses for unfavourable elements in your CV
- lack of tact, maturity and courtesy
- condemnation of past employers
- lack of eye contact
- limp handshake
- persistent attitude of 'what can you do for me?'
- lack of preparation for the interview and a failure to know the background about the firm

The Interview

There are two styles of interviews as far as my experience goes, and that is the private sector and the public sector.

Private sector and public sector interviews usually follow the same 'competency based' theme and format with questions revolving around the STAR acronym, which stands for 'Situation, Task, Action, Result'. You are meant to describe a situation you found yourself in, the task you were asked to do, the action you took and the result at the end of it.

It's all bullshit to be honest, if you ask me, but this is the name of the game and you're not the only one who is expected to step up to the plate on the bullshitting stakes here. If you can throw in some humour along with brass balls and clear cut answers, you will be a few steps ahead of your competitors for the role you are pitching for.

Before any interview begins it's the introduction that sets the scene, and a good handshake, a genuine smile, a friendly disposition and a relaxed manner is pivotal to whether you will succeed. Body language is key and this is how you are judged before the interview commences. You are initially judged on your non-verbal communication before you get out of the starter blocks and first impressions count, so put your best foot forward with a smile, a firm and decent handshake, confidence, don't talk too much and pre-empt some of the answers.

Clear, effective verbal communication remains paramount in today's workplace and solid verbal communication can help us become more productive and build more effective working relationships.

I simply see it as a sales pitch whereby the employer has a problem and I am the solution and answer to it, which takes the pressure off and puts me in the driving seat.

What is a competency?

A competency is a specific quality, knowledge, skill or behaviour a person should have to be successful in a position. Competencies are personality traits that are exhibited in everything we do, and they can be anything from ability to prioritising to team working.

Why use competency-based interviewing?

This standard approach to screening, selecting and interviewing is designed to help ensure that the selection procedure is objective and fair.

Competency-based interviewing (CBI) is used to dig deeper than ordinary standard interview techniques. It works on the basis of how your past behaviour will depict what your future behaviour will be. You are therefore expected to call upon specific examples from your past experiences to highlight the competencies the interviewer is looking for.

How might a competency-based interview differ from other interviews?

Rather than using the CV or application form as the basis for the interview, it will be structured around a number of competencies, each with its own set of questions. As you move through the questions, the interviewer(s) will take you through what each question is asking and the information being sought.

This information will require you to refer to your past experiences within / outside work and will revolve around your own actions and learning points.

These interviews are designed to show the interviewer(s) how you can fulfil the job in question. The prime concern is to find out as much as possible about your qualities. You can take notes to your interview and will be encouraged to take time to consider your answers before giving them. You may also jump back to previous questions if you remember a point you feel is relevant.

An interviewer will be looking at questions that address the following aspects;

- team-working
- ability to prioritise
- ability to work under pressure and to tight deadlines
- working to targets
- desire to succeed and tenacity
- planning and organising
- communication
- motivation
- personal organisation
- action orientated / achievement orientated
- analytical / problem solving

- initiative
- interpersonal
- adaptability
- client focus
- communication
- problem solving and judgement
- results orientation
- developing others
- impact and influence
- innovation
- leadership
- relationship building
- attention to detail
- conflict management

That may sound daunting but in reality your CV has opened the door here and the interviewers know that you have the potential to succeed in this role otherwise they wouldn't have invited you to an interview.

One of the opening questions you can expect to be asked is, *"What do you know about this firm?"*. A cursory glance at their website will usually suffice for this, although I would suggest looking at any recent industry articles that the firm may be featured in as well as any awards or accolades they have obtained to add substance to your answers.

The other opening question you can expect is, *"Walk me through your CV"*. You need to know your CV inside out hence having a copy in front of you as a back-stop so you can't fluff the interview before you start.

Popular questions

Give me an example / describe a difficult situation or colleague you had to deal with and how you overcame it.

Answers don't have to be work-related, although you are obviously expected to link an answer to a scenario that is work-related and you need to have a well-rehearsed answer here describing the scenario and problem, what you suggested as a solution, how you enacted it and the outcome.

If you can't recall anything specific from your CV, feel free to say so but elaborate by saying that you would try to find some common ground and understand why they feel the way they do. Say that you would take a non-confrontational style without involving management, you are both working for the same employer that shares the same objectives and desire to succeed and seek any suggestions and ideas from them to break the deadlock.

A good example that could never be questioned would be to describe a **situation** whereby you were working in a small office / team with a more junior team member who had a reputation for not pulling their weight.

The **task** you were faced with is that you were finding it difficult to get the most out of him and you found yourself thinking back to what your colleagues had said about the individual.

The **action** you chose was to speak to him informally and in private and give him some feedback on what the general consensus was within the team and office. You did this in a diplomatic way asking if he needed more guidance or if he was having any trouble at all.

The **result** is that he opened up saying he was not aware of how we was perceived by the team, that he sometimes did not understand what he was meant to be doing and that other senior team members had taken over the assignments without involving or coaching him. He found it difficult to speak up.

I took this on board and dedicated extra time to assisting him with our tasks as well as giving him more (guided) responsibility. I also spoke to my senior colleagues and asked them to be aware of more junior staff concerns. His work improved and he felt much happier within the team.

Another response would be to simply say that I aim to treat everyone fairly whether it's an internal or external stakeholder and I welcome different points of view in trying to ascertain the best way forward in the interests of the business. I find it interesting to hear how different people see things and that it's a great learning opportunity.

This answer can also be spun in a similar vein to dealing with conflicts in the workplace.

One question you can expect and need to be prepared for is, ***"What particular contribution do you consider that you bring to this role?"***.

A solid answer to this would be along the lines of;

- effective people management skills
- clarity of thought
- attention to detail and a keen sense of the importance of quality service to internal and external stakeholders
- a solid education coupled with a variety and depth of work experience that has equipped me to deal with many different scenarios

- common sense and the ability to 'hit the ground running' and learn new things quickly

What sets you apart from the other candidates?

This isn't a question that you may be explicitly asked, but it's one that you need to have in your locker with a well-rehearsed answer and a genuine passion to complete the circle.

I always like to digress somewhat by focusing on an aspect that sets me apart from the rest, and that is my passion for writing. I tend to pass any employment gaps off by saying that I was working on writing projects via my own limited company. I have plenty of material I can refer to so it's plausible and it sets me apart as a writer and author from the other candidates.

It's worth considering what sets you apart and have your spiel ready to discuss so you clearly know what you are on about. Furthermore, it demonstrates that you have initiative, drive, enthusiasm and a desire to succeed and make your own opportunities.

Provide an example of a deadline you had to meet, how you dealt with it and what the outcome was.

This is fairly straightforward for the majority of candidates and you simply need to know your CV inside out to be able to nail this one with a concise answer.

Give me an example where you have had to manage / juggle various priorities and implement change and make improvements?

I break this down and say that every role I have had over the years has involved having to manage and juggle various priorities and you deal with the most urgent matters first and liaise with your manager as appropriate.

Remember the STAR analogy – Situation, Task, Action, Result.

An example I have used is to describe a situation whereby the quality of work that was coming in from India was variable, as you can imagine, and the task I took part in was to hold fortnightly conference calls to engage with the team leaders and flag current issues and trends as training issues. The team leaders acted on our feedback with coaching, training and development and the result was a 57% improvement on rejected work within 4 weeks.

Describe a situation where you have had to go the extra mile for a customer.

This is a gift for anyone that has an answer well prepared and you need to have one in your pocket, even if it's imaginary. Remember, you don't have to answer these questions truthfully as nobody is going to go to the trouble of checking them out. They just have to be plausible.

These questions either start with, **"Give me an example when / Describe a situation where you…"**.

Overall, answer questions in relation to the job vacancy. This is always the safest way and is what employers want to find out.

Questions that appear to have fallen out of favour are, **"What would you say are your weaknesses?"**. This to me is a meaningless question that I have never been asked in a long time, although one wag that I am friends with says his answer would be that he is a perfectionist. That would invariably prompt a follow-up question asking, *"How is that a weakness?"*. His reply would be, *"I aim for and achieve such high standards that it destroys morale within the rest of the team for those that cannot keep up with me"*.

Don't slate previous employers. Simply give an honest answer as to why you left without being too vague by saying, "I wanted to explore other opportunities" or "it wasn't for me".

Don't lie. Answer the questions truthfully and frankly with succinct responses that cannot be questioned.

Plausible responses can include saying that you were one of the top performers in the team and one of the lowest paid, which was never going to be remedied overnight.

Call centre technology being introduced into an arena that revolved around investigations where you had to give a reason from a drop-down list of explanations if you were away from your desk for more than 30 seconds is another honest and reasonable answer that would be accepted by any employer, and simply saying that you gave it a chance but it wasn't for me.

Any short-term contracts can be wrapped up under one agency for the sake of longevity on your CV and can be passed off as fixed term contracts where you demonstrated a clear commitment for the duration of the contract and exceeded the expectations from you by the agency and their client.

Anything goes, within reason, so long as it's plausible and cannot be openly questioned.

Public sector interviews are tricky ones to gauge and range from the fairly straightforward set of questions that follow a script that they cannot deviate from in the interests of fairness and equality, to the downright bizarre.

One question I recall being asked was, *"Give me an example when you have failed at something and how you dealt with it"*. Other questions posed at the same interview were, *"Give me an example when you failed to meet a deadline and what you did to address it"*.

These questions appear to becoming more popular and employers are seeking an answer to a setback you had, how you dealt with it, what you did to overcome the obstacles and the outcome.

I will be honest and say that it's caught me out in the past and it's something you need to give careful consideration to.

Questions that have no bearing whatsoever on the role are often asked and interviewers will offer to come back to it if you can't answer the question, although in reality it's rare that ever happens and it's just struck out.

One thing you will find with public sector roles is that the more menial the role, the more complicated the hiring process is.

I was temping for one outfit a few years ago in a facilities role which was split between reception cover, filling up photocopiers with paper and replacing ink cartridges, taking in deliveries and just floating about enjoying myself basically. However, as with most outfits nowadays, they want the moon on a stick for washers and decided to turn this role into an apprenticeship paying about £13,000 a year.

I still find it depressing to think there was no shortage of applicants for this role, which was simply a government sponsored slavery programme that mirrors the Youth Training Scheme (YTS) in the 1980s. How we have evolved as a species.

This is a real-life scenario that swallowed up a whole day before the final decision was eventually made (public sector employers know how to stretch a process out). HR in these organisations clearly have too much time on their hands to dream up various scenarios for applicants to address.

However, a few simply didn't bother to attend on the day and I was led to believe that the Director for People, Workplace and Organisational Development was the driving force behind this.

Can you imagine being paid a six-figure salary to design this nonsense? I am clearly in the wrong job here and she is not alone. I recall a temporary worker being paid £66,000 a year by Edinburgh City Council for being responsible for reward and benefit strategies.

The Workplace Assessment Centre plan was set out as follows;

Time	Activity	Who	Other
10.30	Welcome/Intro	Iain	
10.45	Group Exercise	Helen	
11.30	Comfort Break		
11.40	Inbox Exercise	Rebecca	
12.30	Lunch		
1.00	Interview Christopher	Andrea/Rebecca	
	Interview William	Iain/Helen	
1.00	Euan	Sam	Building Tour/Intro to Team
1.35	Interview Euan	Rebecca/Helen	
1.35	William / Christopher	Sam	Building Tour/Intro to Team
2.10	Next Steps	Andrea	
2.10- 4.00	Wash Up	Ian/Helen/Andrea Sam/Rebecca	

Workplace Team – Roles

Iain – Introduction to day, interview x 1, Group Exercise observer, wash up

Helen – Introduction to day, interview x 2, Group Exercise observer, wash up

Andrea – Close, thanks and next steps, interview x 1, Group Exercise observer, wash up

Rebecca – Introduction to Inbox exercise, interview x 2, Group Exercise observer, wash up

Sam – Introduction to team, building tour, questions and answers, wash up

Inbox Exercise – Administrator Instructions

This exercise requires you to consider 10 scenarios that a workplace team may come across as part of their role.

Please outline your response to each enquiry in the space provided. This should either be a description of the action you would take or the questions you feel you would need to ask to understand the enquiry more fully.

You have 45 minutes to complete the task.

Please turn over the paper when you are ready to begin.

Capabilities

Customer	Evidence
Establishes good relationships with customers, treating them as individuals and helping them feel valued.	
Gives realistic commitments to customers, accommodating different needs where possible.	
Looks for ways to exceed customer's expectations.	

Results	Evidence
Can deliver in unfamiliar or new situations to achieve the desired outcome.	
Has a strong focus on achieving results.	
Gives the right amount of effort to meet the demands of the task.	
Is resilient when experiencing a setback.	
Is resourceful.	

People	Evidence
Achieves goals through others.	
Adapts their personal style to meet the needs of others.	
Encourages others to play to their strengths, valuing diversity.	
Manages stress and interpersonal conflict well.	
Has the flexibility to play different roles.	
Listens to others' viewpoints and takes these into account.	

Results	Evidence
Can deliver in unfamiliar or new situations to achieve the desired outcome.	
Has a strong focus on achieving results.	
Gives the right amount of effort to meet the demands of the task.	

Is resilient when experiencing a setback.	
Is resourceful.	

Group Exercise – Administrator Instructions

'Survival'

- Please ensure Participant Instructions, spare paper, pens and highlighter pens are available to each participant.
- Read out the following Administrator Instructions.
- Inform the participants after 5 minutes that they can begin the group discussion.
- If the participants ask any questions do not respond.

Administrator Instructions

- This exercise will last 45 minutes in total.
- You have 5 minutes' individual preparation time.
- The group exercise will run for 40 minutes.
- During the next 5 minutes you should prepare on your own and in silence.
- I will inform you when your preparation time is finished and you can start your group discussion.
- Our assessors will be observing you during the discussion, but will not participate.
- Please read through the information below and make any notes to assist you.

Brief

- You and the rest of the group have found yourselves in a perilous situation as described below.

- There is a long list of items that can be used to aid your survival, but you can only take a small number of these items with you (the number will be specified).
- Your task is to decide, as a group, which items you will take.
- One member of the group should write the list of chosen items on the flipchart provided, by the end of the allocated time.

Any questions before we begin? Please begin.

Stop the exercise after 40 minutes have passed for the group discussion.

<u>Background / Context</u>

On your way back from a holiday in South America, your shuttle flight to the airport is forced to make an emergency landing in a small clearing in the Brazilian rainforest. You and your fellow passengers have only sustained minor injuries but the plane has broken into pieces and the communication equipment has been destroyed in the impact.

Before the plane crashed the pilot had reported a problem with one of the engines, so there is a good chance that the authorities will start looking for you when you fail to arrive at your destination. However, the rainforest is very dense and it will take days to reach the edge of it on foot.

You cannot remain where you are as there is a danger that the aeroplane fuel will catch fire. On searching through the wreckage and the remains of your suitcases you find the following items:

- a guide to South American plant species
- 3 elastic luggage straps

- 6 frozen airline meals
- 4 blankets from the plane
- a pack of 24 anti-malaria tablets
- a 3-metre square piece of opaque plastic sheeting
- a tourist map of Brazil
- 2 large bottles of factor 12 sunscreen
- mobile phone with GPS, fully charged
- 1 litre bottle of the local alcoholic spirit
- 3 boxes of chocolate chip cookies
- 4 current paperback novels
- first aid box
- compass
- flare gun with one fire
- a Swiss army knife
- a book of matches from the hotel

You are unable to carry more than 7 items from this list (items containing more than 1 object still count as 1 item).

Your task is to decide, as a group, which items you will take.

One member of the group should write the list of chosen items on the flipchart by the end of the allocated time.

*

This was all designed for a 2-year apprenticeship with no guarantee of a full-time job at the end of it for a role that was elementary at best and what is commonly referred to as a 'doss job'. A cushy little number basically that only required a degree of politeness and common sense really.

Whilst all of this is laughable, there are some elements that can be taken from here that are worth looking at insofar as portraying yourself in the best possible light to your future employer such as;

- establishing good relationships
- giving realistic commitments (under-promise and over-deliver)
- know when it is appropriate to say "no" and when to ask for help
- being able to adapt and deliver in unfamiliar or new situations to achieve the desired outcome results orientated
- resilient when experiencing a setback
- resourceful
- achieving goals by working with others
- adapting your personal style to meet the needs of others
- valuing diversity (HR love this and it's useful to discuss how you like to learn about new cultures and customs by travel, sampling new cuisine and interacting with those of different faiths)
- managing stress and interpersonal conflict well
- flexibility
- listening to different viewpoints and taking these into account

These are all elements that every employer will be looking for in a candidate regardless of the role that you may be interviewed for.

Closing questions

These are the questions you can expect once you're on the home straight, and the current trend seems to be for interviewers to ask, *"What three words would your friends / colleagues use to describe you?"*.

They seem to think they are throwing a curveball here, and the answers you need to recite are;

1. friendly (indicates you are a good team player)
2. conscientious (they can never spell that but they love to hear it)
3. integrity (this is your fallback position if the job goes pear-shaped and you need to take the high ground)

Recite those answers and you will have neatly covered that off.

Another popular one at the time of writing this is, *"What would you say is your proudest achievement in your career?"*. You are expected to make this work-related as the question is designed to link your highlights with the job description, but this question is subjective and can be interpreted in different ways.

Personally, I like to home in on my writing and finding a passion I never knew I had by virtue of writing a travel blog that was subsequently published by the Shetland Islands Tourist Board and facilitated a private invite to the Up Helly Aa Viking Fire Festival. It's true, it cannot be doubted or questioned and it's an answer that won't easily be forgotten.

I then elaborate by chatting about the first book I wrote and self-published, the popular consumer website I created which attracts a lot of global traffic and guest blogs that I occasionally write for other publishers, writers and the tourism industry.

Interviewers love a good storyteller so have your yarns ready and watertight so they cannot be questioned or doubted, as rest assured, they will be doing Google searches afterwards to verify what you have said.

Questions you ask to close

You need to have some solid questions to hand to close the interview off, and this is your golden opportunity to turn the tables and start doing some digging to find out if this organisation is all it's cracked up to be. Some of my favourites are;

Do you have any concerns about my ability to do this role?

The way the interviewers respond to this question will give you a good indication as to whether you have it in the bag or not. Occasionally, you can expect a question revolving around team work or prioritising your work, but it's rare that you will get caught out here.

How would you describe the culture of the team and organisation?

This is pivotal to me as you need to try and gauge how the team ticks and how the organisation operates, and the way this question is answered will give you a good indication about whether this is the right fit for you. If the interviewers are cagey about different personalities and characters within the team and organisation, you can be assured this is a pig in a poke.

Any mention of the word 'traditional' is one to be wary of as this tells me that the firm is stuck in the dark ages, is resistant and does not easily embrace change and is full of dead wood that wouldn't survive anywhere else.

What is the best thing you would say about working here?

This is always an interesting question to ask and how this is handled by your interviewers will tell you more in less than 10 seconds than the whole interview process. If the interviewers stare blankly at each other and start waffling on about free fruit and 'dress down Friday', you know that you are looking at a pig in a poke. Likewise, if they keep reciting about nobody ever leaving and staff longevity, it's another red flag to me (see my red flags section). The place is probably full of lazy, dead wood that doesn't know any different and are resigned to the fact that this is as good as it gets with no chance of being able to make any meaningful difference regardless of the bullshit that has been fed to you.

A passionate, sincere response aligned with your own values is a sign that you are on to a good thing.

I am seeking a firm that can offer opportunities and longevity, and I would like to ask what has kept you here for so long?

It's a valid question to ask and one that no interviewer would expect to be asked, so it's one to consider. There is a lot to be said for longevity and loyalty with any employer, but equally, we all know that there is no such thing nowadays whether it's sticking with an employer, a utility firm or a service provider.

Loyalty doesn't pay and is rarely rewarded, so why has the interviewer stuck with this outfit for so long? More often than not, it's simply due to inertia and the fact that these individuals are just dead wood who couldn't survive anywhere else or are reluctant to step out of their comfort zone.

Ask the question and see what answer you get to gauge your gut instinct.

Where do you see yourself in 5 years' time?

This is a bit of a cheeky question that I use with caution. If you are sat with someone who has been in the same role and firm since time began, it's pretty pointless. But if you're sat with some power-tripping go-getter that lives and breathes the firm then it's worth throwing in - with a smile - just to see what answer you get.

At this point, you probably know whether the job interests you or not and if it offers any genuine opportunities to progress and develop on a personal and professional level. If it sounds too good to be true, it probably is and one firm that scored 4 stars on Glassdoor and one that slipped through my radar (and was subsequently binned) slipped below 3 stars in that timespan without any contributions from me although they echoed my sentiments.

Who would you describe as your competitors and why?

This is a question that interviewers don't expect to be asked and I find it enlightening as to how enthusiastic the response is. I usually have an expectation in my mind, but it's always interesting to hear what the answer is.

How has this role come about?

This is another one to treat with caution as bullshit flows both ways. The interviewer is hardly going to be honest and say that they can't find anyone with the staying power to put up with the crap that comes with the role.

I recall Andrew saying to me that the last incumbent held the role for about 5 years and moved on to pastures new but failed to say that the one after that only lasted 4 weeks and he passed that off after I accepted the role as a temporary worker. No doubt he will spin the same yarn to the unfortunate soul who has taken the role I binned after 3 months as a temporary worker as well.

Do your homework on this and don't be afraid to 'call them out' if you doubt the authenticity of their response, albeit subtly. I recall an opening line being said to me by a law firm that this was a new role due to expansion, yet I responded by saying that I find that curious as I seem to recall applying for this position on more than one occasion in the past as I have been keen to work for such a well-respected firm. They fluffed and waffled and even admitted that they thought they recognised my name and CV, and that set the scene for me to storm the interview with brass balls and confidence knowing that I had caught them out in the early stages before we even got in to our stride.

The closing question from them was, *"Do you have any holidays planned?"*. My answer, with a cheeky smile and wink at the girl asking the question, was, *"Yes, I am off to Spain for Christmas if you fancy carrying my bag"*. She gave me a cheeky wink on the way out and said they would be in touch. I am still waiting for the phone call!

Other questions that are worth asking are;

- *What opportunities are there for career progression?*
- *Could you explain to me in what direction the company wants to move over the next few years?*
- *What training can I expect to receive for this role?*
- *What do you consider to be the main challenges of the job?*
- *How would you describe the main values of the company?*
- *Will the company provide opportunity for professional qualifications?*
- *Is there anything that you would like to improve in your department?*
- *What development plans does the organisation have?*
- *What is your personal experience of working for this organisation?*

- ***Will*** *there be opportunities for developing my role?*
- *How **will** my success be measured in this role?*

Note the use of **present tense words** here and not hypothetical words – ie, if you were to be offered the job - to reinforce your interest and desire to secure the job.

Finally, thank the interviewer for their time and consideration in meeting you, always delivered with a smile and sincerity.

If you have conveyed;

- why you are interested in the job and company
- what you can offer and your ability to do the job

your work is done and you have done the best you can.

After the Interview

The jury is out for me as to whether you send a 'thank you' e-mail to the interviewer afterwards to convey your appreciation for the time they took to meet you and that you remain interested in the role.

I haven't had any success with this technique in Scotland if truth be known. I seem to think that it's a cultural thing in Scotland to be reticent with your enthusiasm and desire to 'put yourself forward' over and above everyone else.

Some agencies and recruiters recommend it, although I think it depends on the job market and culture of the area you are working in.

It's your call, but it's one I am wary of, knowing that it hasn't worked for me.

Nevertheless, if you have used a recruiter as a conduit for the role that you have applied for, the first thing you ought to do is ring them to let them know how the interview went and that you are keen (or not) as the case may be.

Red flags

Any firm that opens an interview in the early stages by saying that nobody ever leaves here is a red flag straightaway, speaking from experience.

First of all, why does nobody ever leave here? Is it really such a great place to work or is it such a cushy number full of dead wood that's going nowhere? Any firm that trots that out is one to be wary of. I was caught out by that old chestnut when I asked how the role came about – as I mentioned earlier.

Another red flag is a firm that oversells the benefits with the job. We all know what to expect with any kind of role so to sell the idea of free fruit as a perk is clutching at straws by any stretch of the imagination. Sell the culture, not the perks and you are on your way to convince me that you are a reasonable employer.

One big red flag to watch out for is how the interviewers describe the different personalities and culture within the team that you will be finding yourself in. Just watch for the eye contact between those conducting the interview and how they delicately describe the various personalities, some stronger than others and how they interact. Invariably, you will be looking at a hormone-ridden hothouse with mentalists and two-faced fishwives who dominate all conversations and interactions with voices that grate on you like nails on a chalkboard.

An overemphasis on 'work life balance' and how the firm values its staff is to be treated with caution along with words such as 'traditional'. I recall one instance where the interviewer ('Chloe') said that she was trying to initiate change but with the firm being so big with dozens of offices that have their own culture and way of doing things, it was like trying to turn around the Titanic! I overlooked that one simply because this firm is generally well respected in its field and it scored 4 stars on Glassdoor at the time, although within the space of 3 months this score slipped to 2.9 stars and what I found simply astounded me.

Chloe is a shining example of being the master of bullshit who failed to impress anyone above or below her, yet somehow managed to convince the top brass that she was the perfect candidate for the job. She just knows what to say, when to say it and to keep her distance from anything remotely controversial, even if it is within her remit, as part of a self-preservation strategy. A spineless wonder if ever there was one and it didn't go unnoticed as part of my exit.

The Probation Period

A probation period is simply a safety net for employers after the recruitment stage has been completed and spans a mutually agreed duration (usually between 3 and 6 months). Your ability to meet certain performance levels and your potential to fulfil the role will be observed and gauged.

You would expect the tools to be in place for this to be measured, although surprisingly there are a few firms that are not that well organised and they are usually ones that are regulated by professional bodies and the government.

Any failure to meet these standards within that period can lead to an employer terminating the contract without fear of unfair dismissal claims and employment tribunals.

Any successful claim for unfair or constructive dismissal hinges on your continuity of employment lasting at least 2 years if your employment began after 6 April 2012, and 1 year before this date.

A probation doesn't give employers the power to do whatever they want and as an employee, you do have specific rights that cannot be questioned. You cannot be dismissed on grounds that could be deemed as discrimination revolving around matters such as age, sexual orientation or religious beliefs.

Dismissal is automatically unfair even without any qualifying period in cases such as whistleblowing, and you are perfectly entitled to submit a claim in these scenarios.

However, I would suggest caution here as such cases can be found in the public domain through Google searches and you could cause more collateral damage to your own career prospects and reputation if you were to proceed with this. Nevertheless, every case is unique and only you can know if it's worth pursuing for the sake of a blip and a small window on your CV. Sometimes, it's best to just say that it didn't live up to your expectations without elaborating too much and that a probation period cuts both ways, hence you deciding to draw a line under it.

A probation period can be extended if your employer believes that they need more time to assess your long-term ability to meet the required standards for the role. What is important for you here is reading and understanding your contract of employment and to pay close scrutiny to the staff handbook. It's usually quite easy to find more holes in a staff handbook than a block of Swiss cheese as the rules are never consistently applied or adhered to, least of all by the managers trying to enforce them when it suits. This is your first port of call in any job so you can familiarise yourself with common pitfalls such as using the internet, external e-mails, personal e-mail accounts and the usual confidentiality issues.

It takes the best part of 3 months to get to grips with any role and to familiarise yourself with the culture of the organisation. Interestingly, 20% of new starters fail to complete their probation period and that cuts both ways so this is the critical period in any new job. Not only that, but it's a costly mistake if the employer doesn't get the processes right as they are not getting any 'bang for their buck' during the probation period; it takes time to familiarise yourself with the firm, the role and the culture of the organisation.

Choose your boss and not your company. My reason for saying that is because your boss will be pivotal to your success within the company and not the other way around.

You should at least expect an induction programme, procedures, KPIs, SLAs, targets, a structured training plan and specific objectives to enable you to succeed in the role and most firms will tick most (if not all) of these boxes. In fact, it's rare for any firm (especially those that are regulated) not to have this in place and these are open goals if you find yourself being questioned about your ability to do the role you have been hired for within your probation period.

After all, your progress cannot be measured if there are no tools in place to measure it and I succinctly nailed this in one of my resignation letters.

Employees stay with a firm when they are;

- paid well

- mentored
- challenged
- promoted
- involved
- appreciated
- valued
- on a mission
- empowered
- trusted

However, market pressures for profits and performance often take precedent over policies designed to nurture exceptional employees. Having a clear understanding, your purpose and your part in it, being appreciated and being able to positively influence improvements goes a long way though.

You spend about a third of your life at work, happy employees make for happy customers and it's the little things that matter the most.

One such thing that struck a chord with me on LinkedIn in the course of writing this was seeing a connection state, *"Words can't express how touched I was to receive this card and letter on my 1-year anniversary with (firm). There are literally teardrops on the paper! Thank you everyone for making it such a special occasion. I couldn't ask for a more supportive and caring group of co-workers".*

Sarah attached a copy of the letter she received that specifically noted her key achievements and the positive impact she had on the direction and results in that timeframe, complete with a thank you card signed by all of her colleagues.

This has the potential to go viral and whilst it could be easy to dismiss it as a marketing stint designed to garner priceless publicity, it appeared to me as genuine and sincere and was welcomed in that vein. Being valued and appreciated will always reap loyalty and those who feel valued will always do more than what is expected from them.

People don't leave bad firms; they just leave bad managers and this firm stands out above all others for actually having the initiative to do this knowing that it's the little things that count.

Part 2

How to Bin the Job You Hate

Resignation

Remember the mantra: people don't leave bad firms, they just leave bad bosses.

You may have heard another mantra along the lines of, 'if you have nothing good to say, be quiet'. However, if you have had a bad experience and want to enact some serious payback for the failures and shortcomings that you have had the misfortune to deal with, this is your golden moment to speak your truth and throw a few idiots under the bus on the way out. This is your time to shine and be remembered as the renegade who actually said what everyone else thinks without fear or favour.

Bad bosses are renowned for having no sense of self awareness and you will sometimes see anecdotes posted by them on LinkedIn alluding to the fact that they are fantastic managers, whereas the complete opposite is true. These are usually 'liked' and commented on by their cheerleaders.

Nobody likes to be forced to work their notice period and I have occasionally deliberately circulated resignation letters to the top brass before my line manager has arrived at work to make paid garden leave being the only option available.

You can always judge a firm by the way they treat you when you leave and whilst I have had some good experiences, equally, I have had some horrendous experiences and I can be as brutal as anyone when it comes to articulating my tenure.

I wouldn't worry too much about a reference if you're dealing with a large firm as they are centrally generated anyway and merely confirm the dates, any absences and precious little else really. However, recruiters and HR professionals are more than happy to have 'off the record' chats by telephone and frequently do so, which is something you need to be aware of.

If you expect any hiccups on a reference, you can pre-empt it by glossing over it with any agency or prospective employer at the interview stage by saying that you chose to leave by your own volition so any reference can be just taken with a pinch of salt and sour grapes, with all other references 'either side' being fine.

Now, remember the three words at that closing stage of the interview to describe you? The last one is 'integrity', and this is your cornerstone for ripping into your manager and the organisation.

I have provided a few examples of real-life letters that I have written in the past, which are factual, honest and cannot be doubted.

The first one is self-explanatory and led to a showdown with the agency representatives before being escorted off the premises with my head held high. I didn't win my 4 weeks' notice period in lieu because apparently I had brought the agency into disrepute by firing this to the top brass of the state-owned bank who were paying this agency to run a remediation project.

Nevertheless, I set the bar and set the cat among the pigeons. My line manager resigned shortly afterwards as he couldn't argue with what I wrote and totally agreed with my stance. He did wince when I said that I had fired it around the top brass of the agency's client (being the state-owned bank), but I took the view that I should be applauded for bringing it to their attention given that the taxpayers are footing the bill for this folly.

No harm came from delivering that letter and you're soon forgotten anyway. I spoke my mind and my truth and the fact that a few people took exception to what I had to say wasn't my problem. I have always said that the world needs more people like me who are prepared to put their heads above the parapet and pipe up, as there are too many nodding dogs in this world who won't, for fear of losing their jobs.

I certainly ruffled a few feathers and the hierarchy within the state-owned bank had never seen anything quite like it, so they were keen to try and nip any discontent in the bud and find out if I was just a rogue or if I was speaking for the masses. As you might expect, nobody else piped up as these outfits are just full of spineless nodding dogs who are grateful for just having a job regardless of how crap it is.

Nevertheless, when my line manager resigned shortly afterwards, he cited the same concerns I had raised regarding the integrity, direction and overall shambolic leadership from these chancers that the agency was engaged with.

Dear John,

It is with regret that I wish to tender my resignation, hereby giving you 4 weeks' notice in accordance with my Contract of Engagement.

My reason for leaving is primarily due to (agency) reneging on their word in promising an uplift on my day rate if I were to prove myself, which I clearly have.

My experience with (agency) has been disappointing from the outset whereby they advertised these positions at £X a day to entice applicants, only for Robert to say after the assessment and interview, which I performed well at, that the rates are tiered based on experience and I was put on the bottom rate which was clearly not equitable with hindsight. I believe that I was taken advantage of as I had travelled from Edinburgh and it was obvious that I needed the work.

Nevertheless, I chose to give Robert the benefit of the doubt when he said that (agency) do not hold high performers back on day rates if they prove to be performing at a higher level than they are being paid. The fact that (another agency) are paying their contractors much higher rates and are moving them on to even higher rates to do precisely the same work just adds insult to injury.

I mistakenly believed that I was dealing with a professional agency with good morals, standards, ethics and integrity and my experience has proved otherwise.

I would happily agree to leave immediately given that this contract is in its infancy and I would understand if I were asked to do so, although I would expect (agency) to pay me 4 weeks' pay in lieu of my notice period (commonly referred to as 'garden leave'). Anything agreed now needs to be in writing as (agency) and their representatives clearly cannot be trusted on their word.

I wish to add that my observations are in no way directed towards you, and I have genuinely enjoyed working with you and for you. It is simply unfortunate that you find yourself in the predicament whereby you cannot trust (agency) to deliver on their empty and meaningless promises.

On a final note, I would like to take this opportunity to sincerely wish you all the best for the future and it has been a pleasure working with you.

Yours sincerely,

This next letter is more or less self-explanatory, although it's worth noting that everything was (in my mind) going well until week 9 when Andrew hauled me into his office without warning. You would think I had shot the family dog the way he ripped into me, and it was personal. He was just nit-picking at ridiculous things that didn't even warrant a meeting which he had taken on face value from his sidekick, whom he heavily relied on, without even giving it any thought.

He couldn't even bring himself to speak to me the following week and the atmosphere between us was deplorable. I had made my mind up then that I was going to hang him out to dry but I needed to get this letter precise and word-perfect in order to do so.

Week 11 saw Andrew arrange a HR meeting to extend my probation period without giving me advance notice, and that was my cue to spend the best part of 1 hour tearing into him and the HR representative saying that I wasn't even sure that I wanted to stay here anyway. There was no way Andrew was going to support me after I said to him, *"How can you sit there and say that you have had no time to cobble some procedures together when I have written 43 pages in 10 weeks?"*. Their response was pretty flimsy insofar as the firm has undergone a lot of changes. Jesus wept. I put it to them that this is a regulated firm with over 250 years of heritage that has no procedures and I expected much more.

Andrew was so busy being busy that he couldn't even pull together a few procedures together in 6 years of heading up this department, look at Service Level Agreements (SLAs), Key Performance Indicators (KPIs), create a structured training plan, targets or objectives and he was trying to pin the blame on me for not grasping what is essentially a non-job with no effective quality assurance in place, meaning we had to diarise every piece of work we did to ensure it had been completed by the back office function. Can you imagine? How can you measure someone's progress without any tools to measure it?

'Being busy' is the new definition of complacency and laziness.

HR asked what experience I had in writing as I had offered to professionally write the procedures, only for me to say that I have written and published a book about complaining that has ten 5* reviews on Amazon and has sold on 3 continents. Andrew piped up to say that he had bought it and I sent Jane a copy in the internal post afterwards if only to reinforce the notion that she wasn't dealing with a school leaver who had nothing between his ears and couldn't grasp this non-job that I was hired for.

I had lost all faith and trust in this clown and his passive-aggressive style of management at this point so I took my time in crafting a letter that will be remembered in years to come for its brutality, honesty and condemning him and the firm as simply clueless. He caught me out twice but he wasn't going to get a third opportunity and I was going to skewer him for this.

Anyway, the writing was on the wall as far as I was concerned so I had no hesitation in pulling the plug and throwing these idiots under the bus, with garden leave being a certainty as I had e-mailed this to Andrew's boss and HR before he arrived in the office. Andrew arrived that morning oblivious as to what was in store. I said that I didn't know if Chloe had been in touch but I'd put my resignation in (holding the letter in an open envelope) and he treated me like a mate who had said he was leaving the party early. He took me into an office where we were blethering like mates. I said that I couldn't work in this sort of environment where you don't know what to expect from one day to the next, and he didn't realise that was aimed at him and not the office generally.

He waffled on about 'getting used to it' and he just didn't know any different by his own admission. He didn't even know what to do about my notice period (this is a manager with nearly 20 years under his belt in this organisation), so I suggested paid garden leave although I was happy to work my notice but didn't see the point.

He didn't read my letter until we returned to our desks and that is when the penny dropped on his marble head.

Dear Andrew,

It is with regret that I wish to tender my notice, hereby giving you 1 weeks' notice in accordance with my Contract of Employment and probation period.

My reason for choosing to leave is primarily down to you speaking to me on week 9 voicing concerns about my ability to do a job without referring to notes, knowing fine well that I rarely do the same task twice in the same vein yet asking me to take my time to ensure I get the job right first time by using my notes.

How can that be a fault or a criticism? Surely, I should be applauded for taking such a diligent approach to my work and my faith in (firm) as a good and fair employer was shattered at that point.

Having it cited as a reason to extend my probation period astounds me.

You said in the early stages that it would take up to 2 years to fully master all aspects of the role.

It takes time to master any job let alone one with a spec as vast as this, and I do feel aggrieved to have this raised as an issue especially when we do not have any procedures, KPIs, SLAs, targets, a structured training plan and induction programme or specific objectives. How can my progress be measured if there are no tools in place to measure it?

Furthermore, it is difficult to concentrate when the colleague who raises this as an issue ('Louise') is a constant distraction with endless chat and never shuts up talking.

I am appalled that I was given no notice for a HR meeting with you to extend my probation, although I understand that you were told not to say anything to me. Whether that is true or not remains to be seen given that you arranged it.

I expected much more from (firm) and envisaged the principles and ethos of this firm to be of a much higher standard.

It is clear to me that you have since worked to a hidden agenda after that meeting to undermine me, make me feel uncomfortable and build up a case to fail me without the support you promised, and I believe that I have been unfairly treated.

Saying loudly, "Let's see you complete a closure form" is demeaning, unprofessional and frankly ridiculous and I feel that you have left me with no other option than to resign.

I am aghast that a regulated firm with over 250 years of heritage has not left the Victorian age with such an archaic attitude towards regulation with no effective quality assurance in place, meaning we have to diarise every piece of work we do to check ourselves. I have never seen anything quite like it in my entire life and I expected a much more professional approach holistically.

It's clear to me that I can't make any meaningful difference to the way things are done here when we cannot even take ownership of any work that we do via spreadsheets.

A probation period cuts both ways and my experience here has been disappointing for me.

On a final note, I would like to take this opportunity to wish you all the best for the future.

Yours sincerely,

This elicited a swift exit from the office without saying a word to anyone and paid garden leave, although this letter was just the start of an extensive dialogue as HR sent me a letter confirming the paid garden leave with the dates wrong indicating that my tenure had been a shade over 5 years and not 3 months.

My response to this was as dry and sarcastic as you might expect, and I wrote,

Hi Jane,

Thank you for your letter dated xxx, the content of which I note.

Could you please clarify my Administration Statement of Terms and Conditions with the Company, as you have noted that it is dated x (month) 201X?

Whilst it may feel like I have spent over 5 years in that office, as we both know it is only about 3 months.

Can you also please give me the central e-mail address for reference requests?

Yours sincerely,

Jane apologised for the oversight and clarified my dates, only for me to find afterwards that they had got my final salary wrong and did not include my holiday pay. I doubt that would have come to light if I had not noticed, and this opened up the gates of hell as far as I was concerned with a blistering response and extensive dialogue.

I used every adjective I could think of to describe and illustrate my disappointment and I threw in the following words in my dialogue with this outfit; *"aghast, amazed, appalled, shocked, disappointed, inept, offensive, toxic, amateurs, unprofessional, astounded, laughable".*

I asked the question, *"What sort of outfit is this? Perhaps you can answer that question in the fullness of time."*

I never did get an answer but I expect the truth to be flushed out eventually as nobody has ever done what I did and raised legitimate concerns and issues that simply could not be ignored.

This resignation letter was a bittersweet one insofar as the job itself was interesting and the best education I could have ever wished for with a line manager who was again technically brilliant but clueless when it came to managing anyone, with no people skills.

The tipping point for me was the fact that any spot checks and decisions that went against me had to be appealed, which took time, and about 70% of these decisions were incorrect and resulted in me being hammered with extra checks. Obviously, the more checks that are made, the more mistakes you are going to find and it was a vicious circle that I couldn't see any way out of.

Furthermore, it transpired that the hierarchy running this show were having a secret affair, promoting family members and former colleagues from other outfits based on nepotism and favouritism, and were hosting a secret WhatsApp group to collaborate and share information - this was widely known.

Whilst I didn't take my resignation letter any further and it sparked a morning's worth of meetings that day, others did escalate their complaints to HR and the hierarchy were forced to resign about 1 year later rather than have a dismissal recorded on their files. That gives credence to my belief that I made the right decision to leave.

Dear Mark,

It is with regret that I wish to tender my resignation with effect from today's date, hereby giving you 4 weeks' notice in accordance with my contract of employment.

It has been a difficult decision to make, although it is one I have had to take for the sake of my physical and mental well-being which I believe has been compromised over the past 12 months or so working within this environment.

The continual daily changes and demands, unrealistic targets that the majority of staff cannot meet, no QA consistency or common sense applied where at least 50% of their decisions are overturned, the quality of work from Level 2 that takes longer to fix than it would to write a case from scratch, the stress, pressures, expectations and overall lack of cohesion, clarity and direction has simply reinforced and confirmed that my future lies elsewhere.

Working here is like being sat in a car on full throttle with no steering wheel and the salary that (firm) pays simply does not reflect what is expected of me. It's clear to me that things will never get any easier or improve here, and it's time for me to move on now.

Having said all this, I have enjoyed working with you and I have learnt a lot from you and in this job that will stand me in good stead for the future.

It's fair to say that I would not be in the running for roles that I have applied for with interviews lined up without being in the role I have held with (firm), and I am grateful for that.

On a final note, I would like to wish you all the best in your career with (firm) and also on a personal level.

Yours sincerely,

Mark wasn't really surprised when he read it although he did say that if there was a difficult way of doing things, this firm would find them, and he confessed that he didn't know any different, having worked (here) for nearly 20 years. He was disappointed but I wasn't playing with a straight bat here and nobody had any genuine respect for him.

Mark was a likeable bloke and technically brilliant but he had no grasp of the real world having spent all of his working life in this organisation. I can't even say that he had any integrity as what he said to your face and what he said behind closed doors didn't match up, which came to light on more than one occasion for internal roles that I was encouraged to apply for.

Again, he had a passive-aggressive management style and he subscribed to the questionable ethos of the senior management.

'Quality over quantity' was the mantra, yet I saw instances where other staff were simply batting work through without sufficient scrutiny and these individuals were promoted beyond their capabilities by those that were out of their depth in making these decisions.

You were only judged by your output and seen as a machine with no interest shown in anything else other than what you could churn out. Nobody had any respect for him, yet they all had him on their Facebook profiles as a friend. That tells you all you need to know about the culture, ethics and morals of that team that I was glad to be out of. We were all simply passengers on a plane going nowhere.

Interestingly, they immediately drew a line under the 'double dipping' spot checks based on quality assurance getting the majority of their decisions wrong and they did make some positive changes on the back of my resignation letter. This was a firm that always tried to do the right thing, but invariably it was 'too little too late'.

Sharon (senior manager) pulled me into her office towards lunchtime that day after a morning's worth of meetings to say that she had received my letter and asked me to explain myself. I just laughed out loud and more or less said, *"it is what it is"*. They tried to cast the seed of doubt in my mind by saying that if only I had waited, then I would have found the changes I was looking for. Yes, that old chestnut, but my response was *"you don't pay me enough to put up with it"*.

I was given the opportunity to think about it but I had already made my mind up and I had told other colleagues within the team so there was no rowing back on this, especially when I had put it in writing that *'working here is like being sat in a car on full throttle with no steering wheel'* and fired that around the top brass.

I could have changed my mind even on my last day after a leaving card and collection had taken place, but it wasn't going to happen and I can't even say that I was working with a decent bunch of colleagues. The culture within that set-up was rotten and cliquey and the fact that the top brass was forced to resign about 1 year afterwards simply reinforced the fact that I made the right decision to leave.

There is something quite satisfying about 'telling it how it is', throwing a few bodies under the bus and speaking your truth when you have had a bad experience. Honesty is the best policy and occasionally you will be thanked for doing so and any firm with an ounce of integrity will express regret and give thanks for your honesty and integrity.

Useful Contacts

If you believe that there have been breaches regarding the processing of your personal data in an organisation, your first port of call is the Information Commissioner's Office (ICO) and website where you can clarify any concerns you may have.

UK

The UK's independent authority was set up to uphold information rights in the public interest, promoting openness by public bodies and data privacy for individuals.

Their website holds a wealth of information on Data Protection, the General Data Protection Regulation (GDPR), Freedom of Information and register which you can search to see if a Data Controller is registered with the ICO and how to escalate any breaches you believe may have been made.

Information Commissioner's Office
Wycliffe House
Water Lane
Wilmslow
Cheshire
SK9 5AF

Tel: 0303 123 1113 (local rate) or 01625 545 745 if you prefer to use a national rate number.

Scotland

Scotland has its own Information Commissioner who regulates the Freedom for Information (Scotland) Act which covers Scottish public authorities. The main focus of the ICO in

Scotland is Data Protection, and the ICO is the sole regulatory body in Scotland for this.

The Information Commissioner's Office – Scotland
45 Melville Street
Edinburgh
EH3 7HL

Tel: 0303 123 1115

Email: scotland@ico.org.uk

Wales

The ICO's office in Cardiff provides a local point of contact for members of the public and organisations based in Wales.

Information Commissioner's Office – Wales
2nd Floor, Churchill House
Churchill Way
Cardiff
CF10 2HH

Please tel: 0330 414 6421 to talk to the team.

Email: wales@ico.org.uk

Northern Ireland

The contact details for the ICO in Northern Ireland are as follows;

Information Commissioner's Office
3rd Floor

14 Cromac Place
Belfast
BT7 2JB

Tel: 028 9027 8757 or 0303 123 1114

Email: ni@ico.org.uk

If you believe that any regulatory breaches have taken place within your tenure at a firm that is regulated by the Financial Conduct Authority, you are well within your rights to contact the regulator who will have an individual and team assigned to manage that firm's relationship and provide oversight.

This would fall within the remit of whistleblowing and the regulator is duty bound to investigate any concerns. This would be made in tandem with the firm's internal Compliance and Regulatory functions, and you may struggle to get any independent answers or to hold anyone to account simply because the firm's internal oversight isn't an independent function and colludes with those involved to protect the firm's reputation.

Regulated Financial Institutions
The Financial Conduct Authority
25 The North Colonnade
London
E14 5HS

Tel: 0207 066 1000

W: www.fca.org.uk

The Citizens Advice Bureau can offer assistance and guidance on any employment matters, although it's worth bearing in mind that the law differs across the UK and you will have to direct your concerns and queries via your local office within your residential jurisdiction.

Their website is www.citizensadvice.org.uk and you can find the most popular topics on their site within the past month in addition to guidance on employment matters and any other relevant concerns you may have encountered.

Connect with the Author

Want to stay in touch with Scott and be the first to hear about his new books?

Social media links:

Instagram @awriterinedinburgh

Facebook – The Grumpy Git

Facebook – A Writer In Edinburgh

Websites:

www.awriterinedinburgh.com

www.thegrumpygit.com

37997719R00040

Printed in Poland
by Amazon Fulfillment
Poland Sp. z o.o., Wrocław